SP⊙T THE DIFFERENCES
ANIMALS

50 Mind-Bending
Photographic Puzzles

Library of Congress Cataloging-in-Publication Data available

2 4 6 8 10 9 7 5 3

Published by Sterling Publishing Co., Inc.
387 Park Avenue South, New York, NY 10016
© 2004 by Christine Reguigne
Distributed in Canada by Sterling Publishing
c/o Canadian Manda Group, One Atlantic Avenue, Suite 105
Toronto, Ontario, Canada M6K 3E7
Distributed in Great Britain and Europe by Chris Lloyd at Orca Book
Services, Stanley House, Fleets Lane, Poole BH15 3AJ, England
Distributed in Australia by Capricorn Link (Australia) Pty. Ltd.
P.O. Box 704, Windsor, NSW 2756, Australia

Sterling ISBN 1–4027–1203–0

TABLE OF CONTENTS

INTRODUCTION

Do you have an eagle eye? The pairs of pictures in this book may appear to be exactly the same—but they're not! Do you notice anything different? Is something missing? Is something there that wasn't there before? Look closely and see if you can "Spot the Differences." There are six differences between each pair of pictures.

Good luck!

Answer on page 56

Answer on page 58

Answer on page 61

Answer on page 63

Answer on page 66

Answer on page 68

Answer on page 71

Answer on page 73

Answer on page 76

Answer on page 78

Answer on page 56

Answer on page 59

Answer on page 61

Answer on page 64

Answer on page 66

Answer on page 69

Answer on page 71

Answer on page 74

Answer on page 76

Answer on page 79

Answer on page 57

Answer on page 59

Answer on page 62

Answer on page 64

Answer on page 67

Answer on page 69

Answer on page 72

Answer on page 74

Answer on page 77

Answer on page 79

Answer on page 57

Answer on page 60

Answer on page 62

Answer on page 65

Answer on page 67

Answer on page 70

Answer on page 72

Answer on page 75

Answer on page 77

• **43** •

Answer on page 80

Answer on page 58

Answer on page 60

Answer on page 63

Answer on page 65

Answer on page 68

Answer on page 70

Answer on page 73

Answer on page 75

Answer on page 78

Answer on page 80

ANSWERS

Puzzle page 5

Puzzle page 15

Puzzle page 25

Puzzle page 35

Puzzle page 45

Puzzle page 6

Puzzle page 36

Puzzle page 46

Puzzle page 7

Puzzle page 17

Puzzle page 27

Puzzle page 37

Puzzle page 47

Puzzle page 8

Puzzle page 18

Puzzle page 28

Puzzle page 38

Puzzle page 48

Puzzle page 9

Puzzle page 19

Puzzle page 29

Puzzle page 39

Puzzle page 49

Puzzle page 10

Puzzle page 20

Puzzle page 30

Puzzle page 40

Puzzle page 50

Puzzle page 11

Puzzle page 21

Puzzle page 31

Puzzle page 41

Puzzle page 51

Puzzle page 12

Puzzle page 22

Puzzle page 32

Puzzle page 42

Puzzle page 52

Puzzle page 13

Puzzle page 23

Puzzle page 33

Puzzle page 43

Puzzle page 53

Puzzle page 14

Puzzle page 24

Puzzle page 34

Puzzle page 44

Puzzle page 54